I0040384

PRAISE FOR THE LEAN CMO

"Dwight Holcomb has a knack for building relationships and finding beneficial ways for everyone to win. In business that translates directly to increasing sales. *The Lean CMO* is a must read for those trying to use innovation to get ahead in sales and marketing."

Mike Hopkins
Former CEO of Hulu and current Chairman of Sony Television

In 'The Lean CMO,' Dwight Holcomb encourages marketers to re-think tired old formulas, and question the status quo. It may not be comfortable, but it's the way forward. Every transformative organization I've had the privilege of leading— Ariba, DocuSign, Purdue University, Sigma Chi—owes its success to questioning and re-imagining the established way of doing things. *'The Lean CMO'* can be a great resource for any leader looking to get more out of their marketing investment."

Keith Krach
Chairman, DocuSign

PRAISE FOR THE LEAN CMO

"reinventing business requires constantly pivoting and is imperative to stay ahead of the relentless competition that any company with the greatest market share will face. Dwight Holcomb understands that in Sales & Marketing, Executives must take a proactive role to change the rules and pivot in perpetual motion to succeed in a world where technology is advancing at a record pace. *The Lean CMO* is a book that gives Executives the edge needed to understand the nature of this changing landscape. I highly recommend *The Lean CMO* as your next best business decision."

Bryan Stockton
CEO, Mattel

The Lean CMO is a must read for Executives trying to find an edge in Sales & Marketing. In helping the world stay connected through cutting-edge wireless technology, the Executive Team at Boingo Wireless knows that staying ahead of the curve and running lean is the only way to survive and the best way to thrive. *The Lean CMO* shares valuable Sales & Marketing experience, insights and a road map to help Executives understand the best practices of a Lean CMO. Dwight Holcomb has delivered a set of rules for every forward-thinking Executive to change the game and to become industry leaders."

David Hagan
Chairman & CEO, Boingo Wireless, Inc.

"As the founder of Atari and numerous tech start-ups, I know how important running lean is. After years of experience seeing start-up businesses succeed and fail, I know that what Dwight

PRAISE FOR THE LEAN CMO

Holcomb has mapped-out in *The Lean CMO* is critical for any business to navigate the rapid changes we are now facing. *The Lean CMO* should be part of any founder's toolkit for innovative Sales & Marketing."

Nolan Bushnell
Founder, Atari

"Marketing, like business, is always changing and evolving. I always say, "adapt, change or die" because if you're not changing with the times, you're stagnant, and soon you'll be out of business. Dwight's book serves as the perfect guidebook of what you need to do in order to be a lean, mean, marketing machine!"

Jeffrey Hayzlett
Primetime TV & Radio Host, Speaker, Author and Part-Time Cowboy

"My team and I have helped over 15,000 people promote themselves and their businesses. We know promotion and we know results. Dwight Holcomb's *The Lean CMO* will show you how to empower your efforts and get better results more easily and more quickly."

Steve Harrison
Co-founder of FreePublicity.com

THE

LE/AN

CMO

DWIGHT W. HOLCOMB

THE
LEAN
CMO

HOW A SMALL MARKETING

*BUDGET CAN PRODUCE **BIG RESULTS***

THRONE
PUBLISHING GROUP

Copyright © 2018 by Dwight Holcomb

ISBN: 978-1-945255-92-2
Ebook: 978-1-945255-93-9

All rights reserved. No part of this book may be reproduced or transmitted in any form or by any means, electronic or mechanical, including photocopying, recording or by any information storage and retrieval system, without permission in writing from the copyright owner. For information on distribution rights, royalties, derivative works or licensing opportunities on behalf of this content or work, please contact the publisher at the address below.

Printed in the United States of America.

Although the author and publisher have made every effort to ensure that the information and advice in this book was correct and accurate at press time, the author and publisher do not assume and hereby disclaim any liability to any party for any loss, damage, or disruption caused from acting upon the information in this book or by errors or omissions, whether such errors or omissions result from negligence, accident, or any other cause.

Throne Publishing Group
2329 N. Career Ave #215
Sioux Falls, SD 57107
ThronePG.com

CONTENTS

CONTENTS

INTRODUCTION

Marketing is an ever-evolving world

Its tools, best practices, and tactics can change by week. What doesn't change, however, is the value of adding value. In this book, that's my solitary goal, is to help you use my Lean CMO framework to add more value than ever before. And in doing this, I want to add value to you, too.

In the pages that follow, you will find fresh mindsets, habits, processes, principles, and more to take your marketing game to the next level. And the best part is, the core methodology isn't about increasing budget or headcount.

What I've learned time and again is that more people and more money don't always equal better results. Instead, I've come to count on marketing and leading smart. Throwing dollars at a problem often creates massive value drains in companies. So as I share the ins-and-outs of content marketing, distribution, sales, and leadership, you'll learn the primary place value comes from is you.

As you read this book and put the principles to work, make a habit of measuring your results. And assume the Lean-CMO mentality that's always asking, "Where can I get more from what, and who, I have today?" Now, turn the page, and let's begin by setting the right attitude to make big things happen.

PART ONE
BEING LEAN

The Lean CMO is a new kind of marketer with a unique attitude, mindset, and set of habits. Together, they form the basis of what it means to market lean and are the bedrock for the unparalleled results that lay ahead.

CHAPTER ONE
THE LEAN ATTITUDE

Imagine two wrestlers.

The first is a portly, middle-aged man who's carrying some extra stuffing from too many Thanksgiving turkeys. While he isn't in the best shape of his life, you can tell that this isn't his first match on the mat. He's not green, he's gray. Salt-and-pepper hair, smile lines, and years of hard-fought experience. He knows all of the rules, remembers all of the moves, and has racked up some big wins in his career. But when you look at him, you just can't help but think he's a little set in his ways.

Now, the challenger enters. Like the first, he's middle-aged and, comfortable on a wrestling mat. But, unlike the first, he's trim, muscular, and agile. He hops lightly from one foot to the other and prowls around his side of the ring. He's intense, eyes scanning his opponent, sizing him up. However, just a glance shows the difference between the two. While both know a lot of the same things and have similar career experience, the second wrestler is a cut above. He's lean and ready for action. And the simple difference is that the second wrestler lives from a different mindset and set of habits. He's trained for today's bout and isn't counting on past experience to carry him through.

Now, it doesn't take a rocket scientist to guess which wrestler will win the day. The second is fitter, stronger, and seems better equipped for the match at hand. Though both have years of experience, I'd put my money on the second man

6

every time. What's fascinating, though, is that both men have the potential to win. It's just that one of them has done something with it. He's cultivated his experience and skill by putting it to the test. He gets to the gym. He watches his diet. And he's got a mindset laser focused on the task at hand.

As a marketer, I've seen the first type surface over and over. Marketers who are bound by habit, used to recycling the same tricks. The unsurprising secret is that the second type is quite rare. The majority of marketers and sales teams look more prepared for a nap than a competitive test of will and skill. But in the wrestling ring of business, that's precisely where our opportunity rests.

In this book, I'm going to show you how to embrace new beliefs, habits, and systems to blast marketing bloat and become a lean selling machine. It's hard work, but when you imagine stepping into the wrestling ring, who would you rather be? The outmoded marketer who's gooey-soft in the middle? Or the confident contender, focused on the right things, and ahead of the game? And here's some great news: regardless of the size of your team, budget, or audience, you can do this with what you have right now. Getting into fighting shape isn't just about adding headcount or budget, but about thinking and working lean.

These principles will work with any org chart or in any tech landscape. They're the same methods I've used to build my business and those of my clients. They are the best practices for any leader who wants every ounce of value from the assets available right now. Whether you are the chief marketing officer of an Inc. 500 company or the founder of a fresh startup, these tools, principles, and systems will help you get more from less. If this sounds good to you, then let's get to work.

The Lean Advantage

So, what exactly is a Lean CMO? Let's start with a quick definition. A Lean CMO constantly moves, changes, and pivots with purpose. It's an agile person who values sharpening their skill set. He or she is forward-thinking, thirsty for knowledge, and stays on the cutting edge. In short, a Lean CMO always looks for ways to get better, faster, and smarter in every respect.

As a CMO myself, I've had a hunger for these things. But quickly found that the lean mindset isn't imparted from the old-school marketing dispensaries. Lean isn't how business-as-usual is done—*but that's partly why it works so well.* The Lean CMO isn't looking to uphold the status quo. Instead, they're breaking new ground by using fewer resources more effectively. They're people who just can't stop saying, "There's got to be a better way to do this."

It's about an obsession with measuring the right things in the right way. It's about a fanatical attention to detail that finds the tiny tweak to boost close rates. It means listening to the recorded calls from your telemarketing team and rewriting scripts. It's about split-testing your ads and finding the golden formula for your campaigns. It's about optimizing high-performing campaigns to work even better. It's a mindset that knows even when things are good, they could be better; and when things are bad, the game isn't over yet.

THE LEAN CMO

The Five Marks of the Lean CMO Profile

Now, it's easy to think that I'm describing a unicorn. After all, if marketers could get more value with less cost, wouldn't they already be doing it? That's a great question. But there's a game-changing assumption there that we need to shed some daylight on. In order to get more value from today's assets, *we need to believe that there is still more value to get!* The idea that we're optimized across the board needs tossed out the window. This assumption needs challenged. And when done, a new way of doing things surfaces. We'll talk more about this new mindset later in this chapter. For now, though, let's create a profile with the five marks of a Lean CMO. They are always learning, get lightning-fast results, know their niche, reap positive ROI, and run efficient *and* effective campaigns.

The basic reality is that the Lean CMO gets results regardless of budget and manpower. And they do this by maximizing every asset available. No value is ever wasted. Highlight this and come back to it, because it's the snapshot. It's the Lean CMO distilled. And they get there from a foundation of these five marks.

Mark One: Always Learning

First, the Lean CMO is a constant learner. Note that they aren't simply a consumer, but a learner. There's a big difference here. A consumer gorges on gluts of information from blogs, articles, and other sources, but seldom puts this knowledge into practice. Instead, a learner is someone who has a habit of discovering new methods and then field-testing them. They are put into practice, and if they work, added as

9

part of the arsenal. And if they don't, they're simply part of the learning experience. As a learner, the Lean CMO knows that it's not about "winning some, and losing some." Rather, anytime you learn something new and apply it—whether it's a success or not—it's a win. Because you're that much better next time around.

Mark Two: Lightning-Fast Results

Second, the Lean CMO has the uncanny ability of lightning-fast results. Recently, I won a new client just because of this. Here's what he told me: "Dwight, we're going with your team because everyone else told me to expect a three-to-six-month prep period before any leads came in. But your team said you didn't win us leads in a week or less, we shouldn't be paying you a dime!" And do you know what? We didn't just blow smoke. We executed, and that client had qualified leads in less than seven days. This is because the Lean CMO knows that it's not enough to deliver value to a client next quarter—you need to get results on day one.

It's a matter of respect and care for the client or the company. They deserve more than a big, gangly plan that takes months to put on a slide deck. The Lean CMO values results, execution, and then constant refinement along the way. While it's not a blind rush to tactics without strategy, it is about focusing on results and charging toward them right away. Earn your keep by adding value right away.

Mark Three: Positive ROI

This leads us straight into mark three, positive return on

investment. This comes from a hyper-focus on results, and is achieved by doing the right things, in the right sequence, for the right results. Positive ROI is only possible when you have a well-defined target. Does ROI depend solely on a pretty website or clever video marketing? Does it stem from trendy social media posts or display ads? Maybe so—*but they're not the point, they're only a means.*

Again, I tell my clients, "If I don't bring in qualified leads this month, don't pay my retainer next month." Why? Because I'm confident I'll yield results because I know what I'm after. And when you have this kind of clarity, it's your primary pursuit. Throw all the money you want at nifty banners and websites, but are you getting results? The Lean CMO pays attention to the metrics that tell the story of positive or negative ROI. Whether it's landing qualified leads or converting traffic into paying customers, this is the obsession. And everything else is put on the shelf and only tapped in if it's useful to seeing ROI.

Mark Four: Know Your Niche

You may notice a pattern forming, here. Because mark three is only possible when mark four is in place: knowing your niche. This is pretty simple. Who can you add value to right away? Because isn't value what people pay for? To do this, the Lean CMO has done two things: they've clearly defined who they're after and if their company is the best fit to add value to them. In my process this means creating an Ideal Customer Profile (ICP), but no matter what form, the function is the same. Know your audience and have confidence you're the best fit for them. In fact, this by itself will produce results faster than most ever thought possible.

THE LEAN ATTITUDE

Mark Five: Efficient and Effective Campaigns

Finally, number five ties them all together. The Lean CMO knows that results don't come from just throwing things at the wall to see what sticks. They come from doing the right things, and then constantly refining the approach. This means running efficient and effective campaigns. It means campaigns that work without costing a fortune.

In my practice, I've enjoyed success by mixing proven, traditional approaches with modern strategies, tactics, and tools. This has given me a starting place I'm confident in every time, but opens up a host of options to reach the right people at the right time. And to do so with a message tailored to them. This means leading a team that isn't simply efficient, it's effective. After all, few things are more painful than doing the wrong things well. The Lean CMO always balances economy with quality, but can point out where quality is really found. In reaching customers and resonating with them. In solving their problems today because you know that means they'll be back tomorrow.

The Three Codes of Thinking Lean

These five marks are excellent identifiers and goals to strive for. Really, what you have are the pillars of great marketing. And while they're not an exhaustive list, they're the best I've found to break from text-book answers. Now, from this base can discover the path to thinking like a Lean CMO. The right behaviors come from the right mindset. So we'll combine our Lean CMO profile with what I call the three codes of thinking lean." Now, there's a lot packed into these, but together they're a knockout combination. They are: *asking the right questions, understanding true ROI, and learning lean.*

Code One: Asking the Right Questions

Results tell the story of how well any of us do our jobs. For example, I recently hired a new project manager, and she asked me how I'd like her to track time. It's an obvious thing to do, right? In marketing we track everything. But when I took a step back and asked the question, "What do I care about more? Her time, or her results?" From this vantage, it's easy to see I care about results more than time. And in this case, I knew that time wasn't the best metric for seeing the value she produced. So I told her something counterintuitive: "Thanks for asking. But don't worry about tracking your time. I'm looking for the results we talked about together. So I'll know if you're doing your job by watching for those marks better than looking at a time card."

As surprising as this is, it illustrates the first code perfectly. By asking the right questions, we gain the clarity to look for the right things. And if we're not looking for the right things, we can't measure results well—if at all! As of writing this, my team is about twenty people, and I take this mindset with them all. When hiring, I look for people I call "functional specialists." These are people tailored for the seat they fill. And because their roles are well-defined, it's easy to see the value they're adding by looking beyond a time sheet.

You can do this by asking: *What metrics tell the story of success or failure for this position?* Often, time is a component of this.

THE LEAN ATTITUDE

But not in the way we usually think about it. Instead of time spent in their seat, it's timeliness in hitting deadlines and deliverables arriving before my clients even think to ask about them. While this is just one example, it does show the power of asking the right questions. With this mindset, it begins to change everything. From how you run your campaigns to how your business operates. It's a powerful set up for number two.

Code Two: Understanding True ROI

Whether an agency or an internal marketing team, you're usually not the ones closing the deal. This is certainly the case for my company. While we deliver top-notch leads, we're handing them over and not closing them ourselves. This means we need to think about ROI from many angles. It's not simply about our deliverable. Instead, it's about our part in my clients' overall process.

Do you see the mindset difference there? This code is short and sweet, but understanding our part in true ROI is a game changer. Instead of solely focusing on my team's execution, I zoom out and look at my clients' entire process. After all, even if we're a bunch of geniuses, handing over 100 leads per week, if they're not closing, they're not worth the effort. So if this were the case, I'd have to ask myself, "Are we really handing over qualified leads?" And if the answer is yes, then how can I add more value to my client by helping them close? Are our video campaigns setting their sales team up for success? Am I listening to customer surveys and testimonials? These are mindset-checks. They are points that remind me to evaluate us as a partner, and not simply a vendor. Which leads us to lucky number three.

THE LEAN CMO

Code Three: Learning Lean

We've already discussed this briefly, but it's too important to gloss over. Taking on a learning mindset is the capstone of the codes. Because as I said before, learning is different than consuming. So, as you analyze your results, are you assimilating that new information? Are you looking for chances to try fresh tactics and strategies? Are you finding new ways to measure if you can get more from the assets at your fingertips?

To be a learner is to be a challenger. It means being the kind of leader who creates a culture that embraces discomfort. That loves the pain of pushing today's bounds. To do this, you need constant fuel. I encourage my team to become "Google monsters" and constant readers. Then, I invite new ideas, strategies, and tactics to the table. We can learn from anyone at anytime. But unless you're consuming great ideas from thought leaders and fantastic leaders, you're on the path to stagnation.

THE LEAN ATTITUDE

Chapter Summary

We've covered a lot of ground in this chapter, but we've laid the bedrock for the pages ahead. In chapter two, we're going to take a deep dive into lean beliefs and decisions, but before we move on, let's recap what we've learned so far.

1. A Lean CMO gets results regardless of budget and manpower by maximizing every asset available. No value is ever wasted.

2. The Five Marks of a Lean CMO: always learning, lightning-fast results, know your niche, reap positive ROI, and run efficient *and* effective campaigns.

3. The Three Codes of Lean Thinking: asking the right questions, understanding true ROI, and learning lean.

CHAPTER TWO
LEAN BELIEFS AND DECISIONS

Do you remember the 1993 Sean Astin movie Rudy?

It's the classic underdog story of a kid who out-worked everyone to get a spot on the Notre Dame football roster. He wasn't a star because of his talent, but because of his work ethic. Well, I was the Rudy of Arizona State University! It's a Division-I wrestling program and I managed to walk on. You should know, this was the early '90s and the program was brimming with talent. From the head coach, Bobby Douglas, who was also the U.S. Olympic Team coach that year, to a roster full of natural-born athletes, talent oozed from that program. I learned so much there and remember my time fondly. But one experience stands apart from the rest.

Each year the ASU wrestling team helped coach local high school students. We were sent out in groups to answer their questions and give them tips from the big league. However, even though I was on such a high-powered team, I still struggled in some basic wrestling areas. Chief among these was a fundamental move called the single-leg takedown. It's a move where one wrestler shoots in, quickly grabs the leg of his opponent, hoists it into the air, and then tackles him to the mat. I dreaded the upcoming session in the high school, though, because I knew they would ask me how to do it.

The day came to coach the wrestlers. We were in the classic, grungy wrestling room. It had padded walls and mats on the floor. The room was dense and sweaty. The guys in sweat shirts, sweat pants, and donned in plastic head gear. The

20

kids were exhausted because they weren't eating to cut weight before upcoming matches and were expending pretty intense energy. But regardless of how tired they were, they were hungry to learn from an ASU wrestler.

My wrestlers were huddled around me in a group and I was their functional coach. And then the question came, "Dwight, can you teach us to do the single-leg takedown?" They stood, anticipation coloring their faces, looking at me like a demi-god of wrestling. But the problem was that I didn't know what I was doing! I held my composure, though, and it dawned on me. I asked myself, "What would Ray do?"

You see, on the ASU team my sparring partner was a guy named Ray Miller. Ray was a national champion and one of the best wrestlers I've ever seen. He was also a master of a version of the single-leg takedown known as the "low-leg single". So I replayed the hundreds of times I'd seen him do it—*and had been taken down myself, many times in practice.* Then said to the boys, "Alright, here's what you do..."

In that moment, it finally clicked for me. It was incredible. I was able to segment each step, process it, and then explain it. I thought about the problem in a new way because these young wrestlers counted on me. Then, to my own surprise, I didn't just explain it, I did it. I worked through the motions, step-by-step, exactly as I described. And from then on, the single-leg takedown became my favorite move. Even as the "Rudy of Arizona State", I was able to use Ray's low-single leg takedown successfully on competitors who definitely outmatched me both in size and in skill. The secret weapon that came from this experience was that, teaching is a sure way to become good at something you are not currently good at.

Out with the Old: Four Major Beliefs Lean CMOs Must Abandon

This unexpected victory didn't stop with college wrestling, either. When I entered the marketing world, I had to constantly clash with the idea that, "I'm not good enough to try something new." I remember the first keynote I was invited to deliver. It was to an international crowd of 200 global banking CEOs at a conference in Singapore, speaking on how to apply technology in their field at a conference halfway around the world, in Singapore. My first reaction was to say no because even though I speak regularly on technology, I didn't know enough about the subject matter as it relates to banking. I also wasn't particularly keen on flying all the way to Singapore to speak with a room of global banking behemoths, only to flop and end-up with egg on my face. But do you remember the third code of thinking lean from last chapter? Yep, this was a chance for me to learn lean. So, I accepted and then learned everything humanly possible about using cutting edge tech in banking. I did deep research into subjects like artificial intelligence and contacted experts in the field to draw on real-life case studies to use in my presentation. But do you know what happened? I became a subject-matter expert and added value to a group I thought I never could.

I took on the challenge of mastering a subject I had little knowledge in. Then I jumped into a binary situation: *add value or fall flat on my face.* I'm so glad I did. Because just like teaching the single-leg takedown, this experience showed me the value of abandoning the belief that, "I can't do this because..." To transform from traditional marketer to Lean CMO, you will have to abandon some old beliefs just like I did. It's not easy to do this. Trust me, I know. In this section, I'm going to share four major beliefs you must abandon to become lean. As with the other lists, this isn't everything in detail, but as a modern marketer, it's a great start. The beliefs you must wave goodbye to are: *outsourcing means your job is in danger, more people means more ability, more budget means better marketing, and more data means better decisions.*

Belief One: Outsourcing means your job is in danger.

First, I wanted to begin with something most marketers haven't thought much about. And when they do, it can be a touchy topic. The Lean CMO believes that outsourcing doesn't threaten their job. While there are many variants of outsource workers, I'm going to focus on virtual help. These are functional specialists who are skilled in tech applications. I'm not talking about sweat shops where people are forced to work for pennies, either. Instead, these are smart people who work hard and can multiply your results.

To begin, they don't pose a threat to your job. Why? Because they're best leveraged by delegating the minutiae of your work to them. They work best when you operate in the high-level methods like strategy and planning, and they work on execution. This frees you up to do the things only you can do. This means that they enhance rather than cannibalize. Here's the truth, waking up to an inbox filled with completed tasks is a pretty great feeling. However, there's more benefit than getting more done in less time.

LEAN BELIEFS AND DECISIONS

When you work with outsources, you have to communicate with great clarity. You must instantly become a better leader, communicator, and strategist. This workflow requires you know the game better than ever before. Just like teaching high school wrestlers the single-leg takedown, you're teaching the nuances of your field. In my career, I've found the best way to learn is to teach.

The thrust of this belief, though, isn't just that using outsource workers can make you more productive or a better leader. It's a challenge to utilize new methods to drive greater results. It's about getting more juice from the orange than you thought was there. When you take on this mindset, you will become the leader in your space, not the one lagging behind.

Belief Two: More people means more ability.

There's a flip-side to outsourcing, though, which settles us into belief two. More people does not necessarily mean more ability. Sure, adding outsource or contract workers to your team can help. But, if done poorly, it can also hurt. The Lean CMO knows that throwing more people at problems often makes them worse, not better.

Instead, it's about bringing the *right* people to the table. More isn't better; better is better. You'll hear me use this term a lot, but it's about the functional specialist. And this is especially vital for startups. For example, one startup I worked with wanted more sales. So the logical thing was to hire a salesperson, right? Here's where higher-level thinking came into play, though. They already had a great salesperson on the team with a high close rate. But much of his time was spent in drumming up leads. So, we didn't try to find a sales clone to do more of the same. Instead, we found functional specialists to bring more leads to their existing salesperson. This worked well and avoided adding new overhead.

Belief Three: More budget means better marketing.

The third belief is a close cousin to the second, and rejects the old-school idea that "more is better." Only this time, it's in budget. Just like throwing people at a problem, throwing money at a problem doesn't guarantee a solution. Think about it this way. If you're not seeing results, spending to do more of the same will put you out of business faster. Scary thought, isn't it?

Here's the principle: it's more important to be effective and productive than efficient and busy. The quickest path to making this real isn't looking for more budget. It's looking at what's working and what isn't. If things are good, how can they be better? If they're great, how can they be flawless? Remember, better marketing means better marketing, not more budget.

Belief Four: More data means better decisions.

Finally, we all want to be better marketers. So, we should always be on the hunt for more data to analyze, right? Not necessarily. We'll dig into this more in chapter three, but this belief needs to go. Instead of amassing enough data to rival the NSA, the Lean CMO pays attention to the right data. Are you looking at current sources to make decisions? Or are you looking straight past numbers that might already be telling the story? Then, once you've identified the numbers that move the needle, are you acting on them? Marketing decisions must be data-driven. But it's the right data that makes for better marketing, not simply more.

In with the New: Four Decisions You Must Make Right Now

If these beliefs are wrong, where did they come from in the first place? Much of today's marketing is driven by old-school thinking. It used to be about big firms, big dollars, and flashy branding and websites. But it's possible to get better results faster, and with less money. All that is required is abandoning the old beliefs and adopting new ones. I know, because this is what I had to do when starting my company. In fact, whenever you hear something like, "But this is how we've always done it," red flags and alarm bells should twirl and ring.

Instead, to become a Lean CMO, there are four decisions you must make. These are commitments to new ideas, risks, and a willingness to get uncomfortable. The future doesn't belong to the fat and happy, it belongs to the lean and scrappy. The four decisions are: abandon old beliefs right now, focus on results over activities, stop using ineffective communication channels, and be effective not busy.

Decision One: Abandon old beliefs right now!

First, abandon the old beliefs we discussed above. Not next week, next month, or next quarter—abandon them right now! Here's how to do this. Sit down and outline what you want to accomplish in the next 30, 60, and 90 days. Choose which one, if accomplished, would be the biggest game changer, and then make a plan to execute on it. Don't let another day go by without making a commitment to testing newer, more effective methods.

Decision Two: Focus on results over activities.

Second, focus on results over activities. To move forward, you can't operate from a reactionary perspective. Do you spend your days reacting to what populates your email inbox? Are you always too busy to finish your constantly bloated to-do list? If this sounds eerily familiar, then ask yourself: "Am I always busy, but never accomplishing what I need to?" To break from this cycle, look hard at your goals from decision one. What results are striving for? Which will yield the highest return? Laser focus on this. Make it the first thing you tackle in the morning by eliminating distractions and owning your day.

Decision Three: Stop using ineffective communication channels.

Third, resolve to stop using ineffective communication channels. Get the most out of every minute by communicating through the right channels, and logging out of the time-sucks. Are you whittling away ten minutes here, twenty minutes there, on social media? Are you spinning your wheels every hour emailing? Are you communicating with people who are moving you closer to your goals? Make the decision to focus solely on value-creating communication during your work day. This may seem like time management 101, but if you haven't drawn this line, you're not working lean.

LEAN BELIEFS AND DECISIONS

Decision Four: Be effective, not busy.

Fourth, make the decision to be effective, not busy. Don't just make motions, make an impact. Few things are worse than ending a flurried day feeling like you haven't made any progress toward what matters. Every activity should pass this test. *Will this activity drive leads, revenue, and positive ROI for my clients or business? I*f not, it simply has to go.

Expect Resistance

I would love to tell you that the universe will applaud these efforts, but that's just not true. Instead of encouragement at every turn, expect resistance, anticipate pushback against your progress. And do you know who the number one culprit will be? Fear. The fear of failure. The fear of the unknown. The fear of crashing-and-burning. The fear of a bad reputation. And the list goes on.

Just like the fear I faced behind the podium in front of 200 high-powered international banking CEOs, whenever you risk, fear soon follows. But remember, you have to swing to hit a homerun. As you put these practices into action, you'll realize it's a lot easier to be bloated than to be lean. It's much more comfortable to maintain the status quo. In fact, here's the wager I'll make. The very fact that you're reading this book means breaking new ground and forging new paths resonates with you. So put these new methods, strategies, and tools to the test. The alternative is to do nothing; and that is the death of business.

THE LEAN CMO

Chapter Summary

In this chapter, we tackled some of the old beliefs that wage war on every would-be Lean CMO. Let's revisit the milestones, then move on to crafting the essential habits of the Lean CMO.

1. To transform from traditional marketer to Lean CMO, you will have to abandon many old beliefs.

2. The four major beliefs that must be abandoned are: *outsourcing means your job is in danger, more people means more ability, more budget means better marketing, and more data means better decisions.*

3. The future doesn't belong to the fat and happy, it belongs to the lean and scrappy. The four decisions to becoming lean are: *abandon old beliefs right now, focus on results over activities, stop using ineffective communication channels, and be effective not busy.*

4. Expect resistance and fear, but commit to forging ahead by taking action this very moment.

CHAPTER THREE
LEAN HABITS

While lean marketing can get you results fast, think of it as a long-term play.

This isn't a fad or sprint to the finish line. It's a change in the way companies of every size market themselves, their products, and their services. As you use these strategies and tactics, you'll notice patterns emerge. Themes repeating over and over, signaling what people engage with.

For my clients, I've seen this especially with video. People respond well to this powerful medium. So what does a Lean CMO do? More video balanced with long-term strategy. When you find what resonates, craft a road map to help you do it right every time. Create templates and best practices, and *always* sharpen your approach.

How do you do this? The answer is consistent effort. Why? Because it's measurable enough to make good decisions over the long haul.

My goal is to share the long-haul aims of marketing lean and how to achieve them. The key is habit formation. You see, the lean CMO operates from a foundational set of five habits. When steadily applied, they produce results every time. This is great news, because isn't the goal of marketing predictable success? The habits we'll cover are: *always learning, always executing, always filtering, always maximizing assets, and always eliminating the value drains.*

THE LEAN CMO

An Analysis Mindset

Before we jump in to the habits, let's examine the power of analysis. An analysis mindset looks to get better by learning from *both* failure and success. And this can be at a daily level, or even a campaign level. When you view smaller results— *either good or bad*—a lean analysis mindset sees the bigger patterns at play. A bunch of little things add up to big things.

This mindset will be important as you start forming the habits I'll share with you. Some of them will need to look different for you than for me. So I encourage you to tweak and refine as you progress. This will let you continue what's working, and stop things performing poorly. Ultimately, analysis requires you allocate time and stay engaged in your activities. So, before you even try to implement these lean habits, form a plan to step back and put your analysis hat on. Auto-pilot is a button the lean CMO never pushes.

In addition to this mindset, you also need to get your personal habits and life in check. To market and lead lean means operating from a solid foundation. And what is that foundation? Your personal life outside of the office (even if your office is in your home). These are the collection of small things with big cumulative impact. Things like reading at night, getting enough rest, staying in shape, eating well, and nurturing rich relationships with your family and friends. These are the fuel to recharge your batteries; and simply put, the lean CMO needs to be sharp and energized to perform at peak.

LEAN HABITS

Conditioning is Key

As a high school wrestler, it was my conditioning that got me through the toughest matches on the mat. The tide turned for my athletic performance when I adopted the habit of waking up early in the morning and running before the first practices even began. Then, I'd work harder in practice than anyone else. Slowly, my physical baseline rose higher. My stamina was better, my lungs and heart worked more efficiently, and I had a stronger body all around.

On my team, my chief rival was a guy who consistently beat me. He was also my main competitor for a spot on the varsity roster. But instead of working hard just to beat him out, I actually invited him to do extra training with me. I drove to his house first thing in the morning and we'd run together. After awhile, though, he dropped out and didn't want to put in the work. You can imagine what happened next. I got the edge on him. When he was exhausted, I was just getting warmed up.

In the end, I beat him out for the varsity spot. I share this with you, though, to illustrate that I didn't succeed because of my superior skill set. Instead, I was in better condition. I could push harder for longer, and that's what tipped the scales. And it's no different in marketing.

If you find areas you know can work, put in the effort and don't cut corners, you will see results every time. If you're looking for predictable success, here it is. I've won the most fulfilling victories in my life through study, research, and conditioning. Sometimes, the sweetest victories are the ones you've lost three times in a row. I try to instill this in my son, too. So as you look at enhancing your personal and professional life, commit to putting in the work behind the scenes. Remember, the work no one else sees turns into the results everyone notices.

The Power of Habits in My Career

This brings up another pattern I hope you notice in this book. I want you to see that the principles and practices I share aren't theory, but come from my first-hand experience. They are the distilled versions of what I've learned through years of marketing and running businesses in the trenches. However, I haven't always taken my own medicine.

Earlier in my career, I adopted a hyper-focus on results for my clients. This has stuck with me and been a positive mindset, of course. But, while I helped my clients make more money, I realized I wasn't doing a lot of these things myself. This was the tipping point in my career. Because as I saw these lean strategies, tactics, and principles work, my confidence in them skyrocketed. Now, it was a firsthand belief rather than working from second-hand success.

The Five Foundational Habits of the Lean CMO

Now, there are five habits a lean CMO must build atop their personal conditioning, or foundation. They are: *always learning, always executing, always filtering, always maximizing assets, and always eliminating the value drains*. If you just adopt these five habits, your marketing trend will be positive your entire career. You'll simply see more hockey sticks than dips over the long term.

Habit One: The Lean CMO is Always Learning

First and foremost, the lean CMO must constantly keep up with what's happening in the industry. He or she also balances the thirst to learn with the self-control of resisting the urge to become enamored with each new development and technology. There is an endless stream of information and apps all promising to make your job easier. But unless you focus effort on gaining helpful insight while avoiding distraction, this habit can backfire.

As a wrestler, I always studied the tape. I watched every match I could, looking for the slightest improvements I could make. But I only ever adopted what was valuable. In our world, this means paying attention to the best sources of information, reading reviews about new tools, and guarding your focus above all else. Good research actually helps you discriminate against poor tactics, tools, and information. To always learn, you need to be dead-set on its function: increasing results.

Habit Two: The Lean CMO is Always Executing

The second habit is simple, but one few master. The lean CMO is an executer to the core. He or she is the person who doesn't forget the little, uncomfortable pieces of their strategy. The things that need consistent execution and tracking, even though they're not fun. They also resist the urge to put things off.

A leader who executes is simply someone who gets things done when—*or even before*—they need doing. This also means understanding high-value versus low-value actions. What campaign are you driving ahead, and what is the most important action you can take on it right now? Then, you line them up in a plan, and knock them out. Once committed to a course of action, the lean CMO doesn't swerve.

Habit Three: The Lean CMO is Always Filtering

Third, and often overlooked, the Lean CMO knows how to filter out the noise. Data and dashboards abound in today's marketing landscape. To maintain focus, the third habit is filtering out what doesn't matter.

To pay attention to what really moves the needle, ask yourself: *Do I have the right amount of information to make good decisions and delegate clearly?* You don't want too much information, because that means there is wasted effort. However, you can't move so fast that you have too little. If this happens, your decision making will be consistently poor.

Here's a great example: Shortly after launching my very first eCommerce company, we celebrated our first $10,000 revenue month. It was a great feeling and positive milestone— that is, until I realized we'd spent $12,000 to get there! Watch your data points and filter so you can pay attention to the right things at the right time.

Habit Four: The Lean CMO is Always Maximizing Assets

Though each of these habits is critical, the fourth might have the biggest impact on ROI. The Lean CMO always maximizes current assets. This habit helps you adopt a mindset that simply *cannot stand* leaving value on the table. So, you must always be on the lookout for high-performing assets you can repurpose and utilize elsewhere.

This taps into the ability to squeeze the proverbial blood from a turnip. Before you invest in any area, always ask: *Have I extracted every ounce of value from my current assets?* These assets span from tools and tech, to procedures and people. Have you leveraged every resource in your organization to its fullest extent? Or are there still some veins of gold left to mine?

Habit Five: The Lean CMO is Always Eliminating the Value Drains

Finally, we come to the fifth habit, which is closely related to the fourth. The Lean CMO eliminates all things that drain value from an organization. What tactics, strategies, mentalities, and habits consistently harm ROI? Where this gets tough is when you have to eliminate things that go according to conventional wisdom, or even things you enjoy. But the bottom line is, if it doesn't add value, it's sucking the life straight from your marketing efforts.

This also impacts the way you lead. A Lean CMO leads and delegates, but doesn't make decisions by committee or micro-manage. Poor leadership means wasted time, energy, and morale. This makes it the biggest value drain of all. Empower your people to make decisions and get creative with solutions. Then, give them the authority to execute. Not only will this protect your time and energy, it will grow your most important asset of all—your people.

THE LEAN CMO

Chapter Summary

In this chapter, we overviewed the five foundational habits of every Lean CMO. Let's recap the highlights, then move on to part two.

1. Develop an analysis mindset by always asking, "What's adding value, and what's draining it?"

2. Ensure you have rock-solid personal habits in place, including: fitness, diet, family time, and personal development.

3. The five habits of the Lean CMO are: always learning, always executing, always filtering, always maximizing assets, and always eliminating the value drains.

4. By developing these habits in conjunction with a healthy and fulfilling personal life, you're in prime condition to outpace your competition.

PART TWO
DOING LEAN

For the Lean CMO, content is truly king. This means he or she needs a system for content creation, distribution, and content maximization.

CHAPTER FOUR
LEAN CONTENT CREATION

Ever heard of the consultant's pyramid?

This pyramid is how consultants bill clients. The model is simple. You tell people what they need to do for free, adding value to gain their attention. Next, you tell people how to do the "what" you shared previously. This is done for a fee. This is the middle tier, and you charge them for this knowledge Third, and most expensive, at their request, you do everything for them.

This same approach is how great content marketing works. It's about how much value you're adding. The more value you add to people, the more worth your content has. This means high-value content goes beyond informational blogs and articles. Relevance is what matters. In this chapter, I'm going to share my system for lean content creation. Armed with the right mindset and system, you will become a content-creation machine. Even more, your business's future may depend on it. The saying still holds true, after all: content is king.

Welcome to the Future of Marketing

Consumers are more passionate about content than ever before. But it's a special kind of content. It's about relevance and helpfulness. The best content has a long shelf life because it helps people solve big problems. Lean content adds value by solving relevant problems for your audience. This also means it's highly shareable.

THE LEAN CMO

Content marketing aims at creating "evergreen" pieces. These are the kind of videos, articles, and how-to's that add value into the indefinite future. So, why do Lean CMOs love this kind of content? Because you only need to create it once to get lasting results.

For example, creating videos to teach people how to market smart on Facebook is a great niche right now. Simply posting it with a transcript will serve you and your audience. This has value because there are new people getting into Facebook marketing daily. So, if you add value now, where will they come for more information later?

The Evergreen Formula

Notice, evergreen content doesn't need to last forever. It just needs to help people solve big problems to keep them coming back. The formula for evergreen content is that it's specific to an audience and their unique problem, and has a long shelf life. Today, the volume of information mandates your content is quality to cut through the noise. But when it hits those three criteria, you're well on your way.

This also increases your credibility. Gone are the days when people will simply, "Take your word for it." Authority doesn't follow a title or industry any longer. Instead, people will view your content and then make judgments. But, this works to your advantage if your content is high value. The more problems you can solve, the more trust you build. Period.

The truth is while content is king, quality is queen—and

it's actually the queen who's in charge! Quality has many meanings, though. It means high value. But it also means the right medium for the message. Maybe a video is better than a ten-page whitepaper. Or maybe a LinkedIn post is more valuable than another channel. The reality is people who can communicate concisely, and via the right medium, are a step ahead in the quality-content race.

How to Measure Content

Content marketing does bring some difficulties, though. The most important thing for any campaign is measuring success. So, when it comes to content, how do you do that? The temptation is looking at vanity metrics. These are stats like clicks, views, likes, and more. These are helpful to a point. But they don't always mean sales.

Instead, audience engagement is the gold standard. Marketing is designed to get people to take action. When your audience starts a conversation, they have taken action. This can be in the form of comments, questions, or even shares among their network.

When engagement is the key metric, the marketing playing field is also leveled. Think about giant brands with millions—*even billions*—of marketing dollars. They may even have millions of social followers. But, how many of their channels see dismal engagement? Too many to count. Even a small brand then, can enjoy more marketing success than a heavy weight if their audience is engaged and taking action.

THE LEAN CMO

For example, I have a client who's doing great work. So I asked if my company could post a press release about them. They agreed, and the post had great engagement on our end. Not only did this benefit my client, but us as well. This way, we engaged with the audience of our audience. We created layers of engagement and attracted new followers. It also helped show we are a brand that promotes others.

This raises a valuable question: *What does bad content look and perform like?* Bad content is pure sales material. It's all about what a brand can get from their audience rather than give to them. It doesn't benefit them, meaning it doesn't warm up any leads. If you're content is jam packed with nothing but self-promotion, you've found a value drain. Bad content doesn't inspire action, so it just gets ignored.

The Goal of Content Marketing

The goal of content marketing is to create resources for prospective buyers. It's all about problem solving and insight. If you can give people something valuable they didn't already have, your content is doing its job. This means it can give tips, be a how-to, entertain, or anything in between. Great content showcases your authority and competence without being salesy.

Ironically, sales material always chases away sales. If you give people something valuable for free up front, you create ongoing engagement. So as they learn how to do things, the relationship can easily progress to this question, "Can you do this for us?" The more you give away up front, the more perceived value your paid services hold.

The goal here is a hyper-focus on adding value to your audience first. Then, on the actions you want them to take. When you invert these, you have low-impact content draining value from your company.

Using Content Marketing to Get Referrals

Here's another way to think about it. People with a question will know others with the same question. When you answer these questions, or solve these problems, they'll share it with their network. In the same way, as you help your customers solve their problems, ask if they know anyone else who could benefit from your content.

Referrals are invaluable, and quality content is a great gateway. Everyone likes to be the one to help someone else solve a problem. So, when one of your customers can be a solution for someone in their network, you raise their perceived value as well. This means you should create content that showcases you as a practitioner rather than a peddler.

It's easy to sniff out people who're talking second-hand, rather than on real experience. Practitioners have authority; peddlers do not. Where are you an expert? What have you done? What are you doing right now that's working? Great content doesn't mean you have to reinvent the wheel. It's simply the result of adding value where you can right now.

By now, you're likely thinking, "Well Dwight, this is all great, but who has time for this?" Great question. With the right system, it doesn't have to take as much time as you think. Remember, you've already done the hard part: *gaining experience*. So think of sharing your experience as the easy part. However, when I talk with people about content marketing, here are the objections I hear most:

- *I don't have enough hours in the day to do all of the research it takes to create great content.*

- *I can't spend endless hours tinkering with videos and editing articles.*

- *What if I spend the time and money on creating great content, but no one cares?*

Three Secrets to Becoming a Content Machine

So, where do you start? First things first, don't focus on the people who won't care. Focus on the ones who will. Your audience is the person who wants and needs what you're offering. You'll find an incredible ROI when you focus on the people who need what you have. To become a lean-content-creation machine starts by focusing on the right people for the right reasons.

Secret One: Overcoming Fear

The first secret is overcoming fear. You can't execute if you're frozen by fear. The worry that no one will care and your brand will look foolish has stopped many worthy pieces of content from being published. Voltaire famously wrote, "Perfect is the enemy of good." This is great counsel for us.

To overcome fear, means taking the first step. For instance, if you're going to publish video content, start short and sweet. Maybe you can't publish a ten-minute mini-documentary. But can you shoot a one-minute tips-and-tricks video for sharing on social media? Of course you can! And the best part is, look to your existing customers for cues on what to talk about.

Secret Two: Hunt for Pain

This leads me to secret two, knowing what your audience wants and needs. Your job is to become a professional pain hunter. Where is your audience's pain and how can you alleviate it right now? Where is there struggle? Perhaps it's a new regulation, formidable technology, or simple insider knowledge they don't have.

I shared the example of the banking executives I helped to understand technology better. Now, I didn't have all of the answers, but I knew where to find them and *learned lean.* You can do the same. When you identify pain in your audience, do whatever you can to solve it. The best place to start, though, is with the pain you can solve right now.

Secret Three: Know how to Deliver

Finally, secret three is key. In your day-to-day work, you know how to deliver for your clients, right? Of course you do. But in the content world, you must also know *where* to deliver your value. Think about it this way. You don't want to be a paper boy on a route with no houses to deliver to. This is easy to solve;

but it's easy to overlook. If you're going to create content that solves pain, make sure you know where your audience is.

For your content to connect, it has to get in front of your people's eyes. Where are your customers? Find their preferred platforms and create a plan for when and where you want to publish. As you craft your plan, also allocate time for creating your content, editing it, and sharing it.

A Simple System for Lean Content Creation

The best way to consistently create quality content is by using a system. And the secret I just shared is the way to start. First, you need to define what channels you need to be on. Not everyone needs to post on Twitter. If you're a life coach trying to motivate your clients to lose weight, Facebook Live pep talks may be the way to go. But if you're a big-time insurance agent, that's likely a poor use of that channel for you. In this case, LinkedIn will probably serve you better.

The question you want to ask is, "How do I want my audience to perceive my brand?" This perception is what should drive your channel. Video is a black box for many people, but is an effective medium. So, if you want your brand to be seen as competent and clean, you may shy away from it if you lack expertise. However, with advances in tools and technology, anyone can make professional-looking video these days.

While I could share a laundry list of tactics and tools for creating all types of content, I'll focus on my system for video, audio, and written content. These are the three primary content mediums and I've experienced most of my success here. Each of these simple systems works just as well for B2B or B2C marketing, as well. I will share an overview, the essential tools, a few nice-to-have tools, and a lean habit for each.

The Lean Video System

Video can be anything from webinars to interviews. No matter what form your videos will take, there are a few best practices that separate the best from the rest.

The Essential Tools

Good video has two basic requirements: good lighting and crisp audio. If you have these two bases covered, you'll be strides ahead of many. It used to be that you also needed a camera that cost serveral thousand dollars—*at least*. Today, however, any standard smartphone shoots high-definition video. So focus first on your light and audio.

To get these right, you only need a couple of things. At a minimum, you need two lights: one brighter, and one softer. Then, set them up so that they shine at 45-degree angles on your face. This will give you some nice shadows and depth while preventing a dimly lit shot which is what makes videos grainy. For crisp audio, you simply need a clean audio mic that eliminates echo and buzzing noises. If you go watch five different videos right now, you'll notice bad sound stands out more than anything else. So research a simple mic and pick up a couple of lights, and you're set.

THE LEAN CMO

The Nice-to-Have Tools

If you want to take your video to the next level, you'll need a few additional tools. A green screen is nice to have because you can add professional backgrounds, thus creating many different looks from the same space. To use a green screen, though, will require some professional-grade editing software like Adobe Premiere Pro and Adobe After Effects. Next, a high-end shotgun mic on a boom stand will eliminate any scratching noises you may get when recording audio on a lapel mic.

A high-end DSLR or other video camera will take you to the next level, as well. A nicer camera allows you to shoot in higher definition and zoom in without losing quality. It also allows for shooting in lower light or other less-than-ideal scenarios. You can also upgrade with finishing touches like background music and graphics. Finally, you can find functional specialists to help you up your production value. This will require additional time and resource, but may be a wise investment.

Lean Habit

When it comes to video, one of the most time-consuming things is setting up and tearing down. So, your lean habit is to have a dedicated space. Always have your setup ready. This way, it's as easy as possible to get in front of your camera and start recording.

LEAN CONTENT CREATION

The Lean Audio System

Audio has long been a powerful content medium. Today, podcasting and other forms are gaining in popularity over radio. And the good news is, it's easier than ever to start.

The Essential Tools

The bar for recording basic audio is far lower than ever before. Just like video, today's smartphones have decent-quality microphones in them. This allows you to record passable audio in quiet environments. You can also purchase inexpensive microphones that plug directly into your computer's USB port.

The Nice-to-Have Tools

Once you've recorded audio lean and proven its value, the next step is upgrading to a high-end digital recorder, an amplifier for your smartphone, or quality mic. Because this tech develops so rapidly, I suggest you do some research on what brands and models work best.

Lean Habit

Often, editing your audio is what takes the most time. So, a pro-tip is to have a place to take notes while you're recording. This way, if you make a mistake, you can simply mark down when it happened to fix it in less time.

THE LEAN CMO

The Lean Writing System

Finally, we have the most famous and abundant form of content: writing. It has been around the longest and doesn't appear to be going anywhere fast. It's certainly still viable. It's also the lowest-barrier-to-entry. So if you're brand new to content marketing, this is a perfect place to dip your toe in the water.

The Essential Tools

For written content, the most essential tool is actually a consistent schedule. Believe it or not, inconsistency in post frequency is what scatters an audience most. To start, you'll need at least two designated dates: a creation date, and a posting date. For example, clear your schedule to write every Monday afternoon, and then schedule the post for Friday at 3 p.m. Whatever the frequency you're aiming for, don't set the bar so high that you can't keep up the pace.

The Nice-to-Have Tools

Beyond creating the content, visuals and social posts are excellent upgrades. Images, graphics, and videos related to your content help make it more engaging. And quotes make it more sharable. These will ultimately help you deepen engagement and broaden your reach. Though they're not absolute necessities, they do make a positive impact.

Lean Habit

The lean writing habit is simple: whether you write every day, or once per month, stay consistent. Set a long-term posting schedule and keep it up. Don't let inconsistency crumble the audience you will build.

Where to Begin

I've shared a lot of information in this chapter. If you're new to content marketing, it may feel overwhelming. So, I'll leave you with a final point of guidance before we move on. When you're crafting your content strategy, study what the high-level thought leaders in your field are doing. How are they perceived? What channels are they active on? What mediums do their audiences engage with most?

When you identify these patterns, you're flexing your lean learning muscles rather than going in blind. This way, you can catalyze capitalize on someone else's success. Just like me watching hours of wrestling film before matches, do your homework on what works in your industry. Then, pattern your initial efforts after what you learn.

THE LEAN CMO

Chapter Summary

In this chapter, I shared my secrets and system for how to become a lean-content machine. Before we discuss how to distribute your content, let's review what we learned.

1. Creating quality, evergreen content is the future of marketing, and a great way to engage your audience.

2. Quality content adds value before asking for a transaction.

3. The three secrets to becoming a content machine are: *overcoming fear, hunting for pain, and knowing how to deliver your content.*

4. Develop systems, or use the ones I shared, for creating quality video, audio, and written content in less time and with better results.

CHAPTER FIVE
LEAN CONTENT DISTRIBUTION

There is a perfect recipe for the secret sauce of content marketing.

t's a special blend of creation and distribution. But the mix of those all-important ingredients might surprise you. At this point, you've established lean habits and understand how to create quality content. But the most important ingredient is still missing: distribution.

The truth is you can create the best content in the world, but it's only as valuable as the engagement it generates. And it can't engage people who never see it. After all, what's the difference between a video sitting on my desktop and one unwatched on an irrelevant channel? Not much. The age-old 80/20 principle applies here. Content marketing is 20 percent creation, and 80 percent distribution.

While it's important to have a message, it's even more important to get it out. Distribution is often missed by folks new to content marketing. So, in this chapter I'll explain some of the Lean CMO's content distribution secrets and add more insight into measuring ROI.

Avoiding the Content Graveyard

Sometimes people think the magic of distribution is only available to genius marketers with PhDs. The great news, however, is that's not the case. The Lean CMO can distribute content effectively without fancy degrees or silver bullets. Getting your content in front of the right people is what I call "avoiding the content graveyard." And to do this involves three considerations: *channels, consistency, and frequency.*

For starters, the content graveyard is the sad place where great content goes to die. This means you've put in all the work we discussed in the last chapter, but you're not going to reap the reward. Why? Because you lack the right methods of distribution. The graveyard means your content goes unseen and lacks engagement.

Fortunately, there is a solution. And it involves eliminating the content graveyard from the start. As they say, an ounce of prevention is worth a pound of cure. To begin, let's look at how to determine the right channels.

Channels

Channels refer to specific platforms you can share content on. This includes everything from social media to your own website to email. The toughest part is the sheer volume of channels today. If you tried to publish to every channel, you'd have a full-time job dedicated to busy work. Instead, you want to strategically choose the channels where your target audience spends time.

For example, if you're selling software in the legal industry, and your target customers primarily hang out on legal blogs or LinkedIn, that should be the channel you focus on first. Choosing the right channel focuses your efforts. It also narrows the scope of best practices and platforms you need to learn. The quickest way for your content to end up in the graveyard is by using the wrong channels.

LEAN CONTENT DISTRIBUTION

When choosing channels, imagine yourself at a tradeshow. Where are the people gathering? Where are conversations happening? Where is your industry's water cooler? This is where you want to be. To identify these, there's a small amount of leg work involved. First, take a look at where industry leaders are gaining engagement. And how they're doing it. This is a quick study for both location and best practices. What content makes your audience respond? And what is a gathering place for crickets? Remember, follow engagement as your primary metric.

Consistency

Consistency is the next consideration. When you find the right channels, you need to establish a consistent presence. People must be able to count on regular value from you. Today, memories fade quickly, so if you're not top-of-mind, you may as well not exist. While some content is better than no content, an empty following with a few scattered posts damages your credibility.

For example, have you ever seen a company's social presence with a few posts that are years old with no recent activity? What's your first thought, "Are these guys still in business?" Consider this, how much value does an empty, or irregular, channel have for your audience? Very little. The Lean CMO measures success by engagement, and engagement follows value.

Frequency

Frequency is closely related to consistency. Really, it's an extension of it. You may publish an excellent piece of evergreen content. However, if it's followed by sporadic activity—or worse still, no activity—you're simply building headstones in your own content graveyard. You don't want to be a one-off. However, there's a flip side. If you post a deluge of content that's too much for people to digest, you'll run your audience off. To become a known entity in your space means adding consistent value by solving problems with Goldilocks frequency; not too much, not too little, just right.

To find your sweet spot, start with a similar schedule to those who are doing a great job in your field. Do they post their own content once-per-week and then share three industry articles with commentary? Or do your people respond well to a deep, very thorough whitepaper or video published once-per-month? There is no one-trick-pony approach, here. Instead, it's audience driven.

How to Properly Measure ROI

The number one question the Lean CMO needs to answer is this: "Are we seeing positive ROI from these efforts?" If not, it's time to cut them out or pivot. In my wrestling days, if I put in tons of effort into an exercise program that was ineffective, or even negatively impacted my performance, I'd have been crazy to keep doing it. Distribution is the same way. So, what's the best way to measure ROI for your content marketing? I'll share my top three methods for measuring ROI: *conversion rates, quality analytics, and engagement.*

LEAN CONTENT DISTRIBUTION

Conversion Rates

The goal of content marketing is engagement. And the goal of engagement is converting followers to customers. These may seem obvious, but conversions are key. Simply put, if you have 100 people viewing a product on your website, and one of them buys, you have a one-percent conversion rate. This isn't great.

Carefully measuring each different element impacting what helps people to take a desired action, or "convert" will help you identify what problem exists and give clues as to what can be done to improve the conversion rates. Why aren't more people converting? Is it poor copy or an unclear product description? Or perhaps it's a step further back. Does the content or ad driving people to this page accurately set people up to purchase? Or do they seem unrelated? Is there a clear Call-To-Action (CTA)? Is the CTA commensurate with the perceived return that your prospect will get for taking the action? Conversions can be more than purchases, as well. Maybe you're trying to get people to book meetings or fill out a form. A conversion measures the action you want people to take.

Quality Analytics

Next, insight into your audience's activity is only as good as your analytics. There are a wide variety of tools for analytics. They include website metrics, social media stats, email rates, and more. Everything in the digital environment can be measured. And what can be measured can be improved.

THE LEAN CMO

In general, you want your analytics to tell you a few things every time:

- What action was performed?
- Who performed it?
- Where did they come from?
- What is their profile: age, gender, industry, income, company, number of employees, job title, industry, annual revenue, etc.?

Now, you can go much deeper down the analytics rabbit hole than these. But armed with these data, you can identify what traffic is the most valuable. And on top of that, which referring channels they are most likely to convert from. For example, if your goal is to set prospect appointments through a campaign that drives traffic to a landing page with a CTA to fill-out a form to schedule a free consultation to learn more about your service or offering and you have a 10% conversion rate, you might try running an A|B split test by using a duplicate landing page with messaging crafted directly to a specific industry vertical. Then, after adjusting the search criteria to include this industry and also consider targeting the best job title for those decision makers who have the right authority to approve your proposal, run the test, comparing the results between the two landing pages. What you will probably find is that even though the search audience will be smaller with the industry-specific page, you'll probably get more traffic, a higher-conversion rate and a better fit prospect who that will also increase your closing ratio. The next step is to rinse and repeat this method for any other industries your serve.

LEAN CONTENT DISTRIBUTION

By speaking directly to a hyper-targeted market segment, they feel that your solution has been designed specifically for them which helps the sales process feel more organic for your prospects.

Engagement

By now, I may sound like a broken record. But measuring engagement is not only important, it's tricky. As I said before, engagement is more than clicks, likes, or shares. Engagement is a next-step action beyond passive consumption. It's not enough for people to consume your content. You want them to act on it in a way that leads them closer to conversion. Here's an example of how I measure my engagement.

Recently, I've run a lot of LinkedIn connection campaigns. My goal is straightforward. I want to connect with specific types of people, and then use a series of scripts to invite them to book appointments. For these campaigns, then, a conversion is booking the appointment. Strategically, there are a few steps that lead up to that. So my first measure of engagement is, "Do they respond to my connection request?" Pretty simple so far. Next, do they respond to my initial script—and then those thereafter.

Engagement is when your audience take a pre-defined step toward conversion. So, as you view your success and failure, you can start to do more of what works. You'll see patterns from the most effective days of the week, to the best times to invite people to engage. These will vary by vertical and location. However, I've saved the best for last.

THE LEAN CMO

The number one rule of engagement is known as, "Speed to lead." You want to respond as quickly as possible to people who engage. You have their interest and attention, so capitalize on it immediately and draw them closer to conversion.

At the end of the day, the goal of marketing is bringing in more dollars than are expended. So, as you analyze your data and tweak your efforts, always keep a focus on sales. If you're not closing deals, you're wasting value. The Lean CMOs career mission is maximizing value, so pivot when you find the value drains, and double-down when you find something that works.

LEAN CONTENT DISTRIBUTION

Chapter Summary

In this chapter, I shared the fundamentals of content distribution, as well as measuring ROI. Let's review the main takeaways before moving on to part three, *Leading Lean.*

1. The perfect recipe for content marketing success is the right mix of content creation and distribution—which is usually 20 percent creation, and 80 percent distribution.

2. The first objective of distribution is to avoid the content graveyard by using the right channels, consistency, and frequency to create engagement.

3. When measuring ROI, focus on these three elements: conversion rates, quality analytics, and engagement—without them, you cannot effectively measure ROI.

4. At the end of the day, marketing is about increasing sales; so ensure everything you do invites your audience one step closer to conversion by doing more of what works, and less of what doesn't.

PART THREE
LEADING LEAN

The Lean CMO works proven strategies and processes to create audience engagement. But they don't just stop there. The hallmark of the Lean CMO is the ability to lead both internal and external teams in doing so, as well.

CHAPTER SIX
LEAN SELLING

Sales is simple when approached the right way.

Gimmicks only get you so far, and other sales systems turn deals into complex messes. Lean selling is different. It's not fancier, and certainly not more complicated. Instead, it's a common-sense approach to working with people. At its core, lean selling is about finding a way to add more value to everyone at the table. The Lean CMO identifies and designs win-win scenarios by following three simple principles, which I'll share with you in this chapter.

Right Prospect, Right Deal, Right Time

Lean selling starts with breaking down your entire sales process into individual pieces. From there, analyze them and ensuring each is executed in the best way possible. I always begin with what I call the *ideal customer profile* (ICP). It's an outline of my ideal prospect that helps me identify who is a fit for us, and who are we the best fit for. It took a while for me to "get it," but I now know that if I have the wrong target, I'll waste a lot of time and resources.

Fundamentally, lean selling means closing the right deal, at the right time, with the right prospect. Tools like the ICP help me identify the right prospect. But I also have to find the right deal, which always involves a lot of up-front questions. As an example, here's a situation that may sound familiar.

THE LEAN CMO

You meet a prospect and discuss a potential project. You're an excellent fit for their needs, and the work is right up your alley. You've spent more than an hour discussing details and even sparking ideas for them. You're adding value to the prospect from the start; a great way to begin a client relationship. However, as the meeting draws to a close you learn that while the prospect may be a great fit, the deal and timing are miles away. Instead of being ready to start, you learn the prospect is shopping vendors, and six months to a year from any decision.

If you're like me, that last part probably made you cringe. However, the Lean CMO can avoid this situation with a few well-placed questions. Four of the most fundamental questions for any sale is:

1. *What's your decision-making process?*

2. *What's your timeline?*

3. *What's your budget?*

4. *How do you see us helping you?*

When you're armed with this information, then you can answer their most important question: "Can you deliver on time and at budget?"

This tactic is called pre-qualification. The idea is to know you're going after the right people before you invest even a penny in marketing to them. In fact, you can even get some to qualify themselves for you. For example, knowing a company's revenue range can tell you a lot about their potential fit. If they're a startup bringing in $10,000 per month, but your retainer starts at $7,500, you know the numbers won't add up. Pre-qualification saves both sides a lot of time and energy. If you talk to the wrong people, it's going to hurt you in the long run.

Fundamentally, though, finding the right deal, at the right time, with the right prospect rests on how you answer this question: "Will this client become a success story for me?" If not, pass on the deal, or be wary walking into it. The best deals are the ones you can solve with certainty. This way, you set yourself up to collect excellent customer testimonials (on video if you can!).

The House On-Fire-Sales Method: "Closing" is a Myth!

When you've done the up-front work right, closing becomes a myth. Instead, there's a natural conclusion to what you've discussed. Part of what I do is coach salespeople. One of the most common questions I field from them is, "How should I handle when prospects say, 'Let me think about it,'?" If I know their prospect has real pain, and the person I'm coaching has a legitimate solution, I tell them to imagine this scene.

Picture your house is on fire, and you're standing in the front lawn. The fire department is miles away, and you're on your own. Then, someone walks up to you with a fire hose and offers to sell it to you. Obviously, there's no need for a close and no decision to make. You have acute pain and this person has the only solution.

THE LEAN CMO

Now, imagine this scene a second time. Your house is on fire and the same person brings the fire house to your front lawn, ready to sell it to you. However, instead of paying for it and saving your house, you haggle over the price, dig in your heels on minutiae, and put off signing the contract.

We all know the second scenario presents a poor client. The close disappears when you have the right deal, at the right time, with the right prospect. So, if you're bottle-necking on the contract or other minutiae, re-evaluate those three indicators.

Another thing to consider, is that some people are just not a fit and it's better to find out early and move on. In our case above, if your house is drenched from a fresh downpour of rain and there is no sign of any fire, the person with the water hose will be best-served to move on down the block to the next house to seek out those who actually have a fire and are in need. Your house is soaked. You do not need a water hose, so why waste time where there is no need? Learning this lesson is critical to minimizing time-wasting sales calls that have no natural fit.

Lastly, if a client says, "Let's do this!", do you say, "Great, I'll send you the contract. Please let me know if you have any questions. Thank you. Good bye." Or, do you say, "Great, I've just sent you the contract via e-mail, did you get it? ...okay great! Now just scroll to the last page. Do you see the digital signature block? Perfect! Now, just place your digital signature there and we're all set. I'll walk your signed agreement to our on-boarding team right now. Thank you for your business and welcome aboard!". See the difference?

LEAN SELLING

The Strategies of Lean Selling

When you begin selling lean, it's helpful to keep what Stephen Covey says about sales relationships in *The Seven Habits of Highly Effective People*. He writes, "First seek to understand, then to be understood, then to find a win-win solution." You should notice another pattern in the lean methodology, here.

The Lean CMO always looks to identify their audience's pain before offering a service. This is true in content marketing, but it's also true in sales. To begin, ask questions and seek to understand the prospect. Get curious about things like their successes and what their company does well. Find out how they win with their clients.

This opens the door to discover what they're doing, how they're doing it, and how much they're paying for it. From here, you have ammo to address the deal in specific terms. But one of my favorite questions at this stage is to ask this question, "Can you share your expectations for what you'd like to get out of this?" Then, once they tell you what they're hoping for, do it!

I'll end this chapter with a few closing points to remember for improving the sales process. Following a consultative sales process is always best since you are beginning the relationship by asking questions and learning about who they are, not dumping on them with all of your impressive abilities and track record. Throughout the process, make mini-contracts with your prospect. Constantly get their buy-in on each step of the sales process. "First, I need to learn more about your company to determine if there is even a fit for us to do business together. Is that okay with you?" Get their permission to move forward in the direction you need to go to run an impactful conversation. Speak like a normal human being. Eliminate sales-speak wherever you can. Stop starting calls by saying, "Hi, how are you today?" It smacks of a sales call and if you are going to interrupt their day, give them the courtesy of getting to the "Why" they should care and listen further. Instead of asking how they are, ask if you've caught them at a bad time. Give them a chance to let you in. Don't "show up and throw up". Most importantly, at the very beginning of any sales effort, create your Ideal Customer Profile (ICP). Map out an avatar of who this person is and where they hang out. I highly recommend Geoffrey Moore's "Crossing the Chasm" to establish a "beach head" and move purposefully at this hyper-defined target.

To sell lean means understanding exactly who you're talking to, what they want, and being able to articulate how you can solve that pain. While there are an endless number of strategies and tactics we could fill another book with, that simple premise will serve you well. Remember, the Lean CMO closes the right deal, at the right time, with the right prospect.

LEAN SELLING

Chapter Summary

In this chapter, you learned the basics of lean selling. Let's review the principles discussed and enter into our final chapter on leading lean.

1. Lean selling is about closing the right deal, at the right time, with the right prospect.

2. The right deal is one each party can benefit from.

3. The right time is when the decision and project start date are advantageous to your cash flow and production schedule.

4. The right prospect is the one who has a problem you can solve and values what you bring to the table

CHAPTER SEVEN
LEADING LEAN

If you struggle to lead well, your teams will struggle to perform.

or your company to reap the full benefit of a truly Lean CMO, you need to embody a set of lean leadership qualities. And what you'll find is that it's easy to point out flaws in others. Great leaders have a keen eye for opportunities to improve. However, the best will always turn this critical eye on their own performance first. In this chapter, I'll share how to do this. And also, the impact it will have on your team.

The Challenges of Leading Lean

The Lean CMO leads holistically. This means fully integrating him or herself, the internal team, and the external team or contractors. Whenever I work with new people, I know I have to do two things. First, I have to trust them. And second, I have to give them enough authority to do their job. When I do this, it ensures I'm not turning them into a widget I plug into a work machine. This mandates I respect their skill set, experience, and invite their opinion. (This is especially beneficial to offshore working relationships.)

This is more than a nice way to lead, as well. It's effective. You see, leading lean requires rock-solid delegation. This means both trust and buy-in must be present in high volume. They are precious assets to maximize.

90

THE LEAN CMO

In my CEO network, I have three peers who try to do everything themselves. Without fail, they become stressed near to physical exhaustion. Often, leaders at the c-level get stuck on micro-managing and control. However, what they miss is the first secret of leading lean: *focus on reviewing, not doing.*

The key is to do "a lot" with "a little" by getting increased productivity from your team. No matter how big or small, lean leadership is about unlocking the potential for more. By the focus on reviewing, what you're emphasizing is results rather than control. In this way, you're also analyzing what's working, and what isn't. So your work goes toward optimization rather than tasks.

When I Lead Lean

I'll share an example to illustrate. One of my clients needed a better way to run customer meetings to demonstrate their product. To date, their format was offering a snoozer of a demo via WebEx. These demos were fraught with bugs and saw poor engagement. So at the end of each meeting, they saw a mass exodus of potential customers.

Now, putting on your lean analysis hat, you'll notice a few things. First, they were doing the leg work of demoing their product to every single prospect. This meant they sunk considerable time into scheduling, demoing, and then following up. It also meant they weren't certain if they had the right prospect at the right time—*a chief principle of lean selling.*

So the problem to solve wasn't simply, "How can they do

customer demos better?" It was, how can we add more value to their prospects? How can we pre-qualify warm leads? And how can we do so while freeing up their time to focus on higher-value activities? But, conventional sales wisdom teaches there's no better way to spend time than with prospects, right? So what does the Lean CMO do from here?

I quickly saw the solution was to make a simple, ten-minute demo video prospects could watch on-demand. This would create a higher-quality experience for their prospects. It would also free up their time to work on more valuable things. Case closed! All I had to do was execute on my side and watch their sales flow in. Wrong.

While I helped my clients solve a problem lean, I jumped right into "doing." I created the video and slipped straight into doing all of the editing, graphics, music, and the rest. All of the details were on me. And while I can do the legwork of video, it's a black hole of effort for me. I'm not a functional specialist, so I'm inefficient. I'd rolled up my sleeves to get the work done, but this meant I was up editing until five a.m. for three days straight. After hitting the point of exhaustion, I realized I couldn't keep doing this.

Prices for video editing sub-contractors have come down so much, I was able to hire someone to knock out the work in less than a day. She did a great job because I'd done the prep work up front. All I had to do was provide clear direction to set her up for success. I made money, my contractor made money, and so did my client. So, the lean leader can't simply help everyone else adopt a lean mindset. He or she must lead themselves first. The best part about this, is that leading this way and having great results caused my client to become an evangelist, who then shared this experience with others. It wasn't long before I was being pursued by others looking to have the same results.

Leading Yourself

As the leader, you set the tone and model for how your company works. Follow the leader isn't just a kids' game— it's how culture works. So, your people will emulate you. It's too easy to dole out your medicine to others without taking it yourself. This means leading lean starts with you.

How do you do it? If these are new concepts to you, here's a quick way to start. Think about your current workload. What tasks do you do over and over? What emails do you send with roughly the same content? These areas are perfect candidates for templates and processes. When you stop and take the time to process-out your work, your people catch on. Do you know what a boost in efficiency this is even in a small company? It saves effort and energy to the tune of thousands each year. And for bigger companies, each month.

The leader is truly the ceiling for growth. This means as you grow, so do your people. To keep growing, I hold myself to three principles: *discipline, asking the right questions and inviting the right perspective, and accountability.*

LEADING LEAN

Discipline

First, your people will only work as hard as you do. We all have days we're tempted to be lazy. We want to put off the hard, uncomfortable things. But when this becomes a habit, the wheels rattle off. When you stay disciplined, you ensure things are executed on. I've found a great gut check is when I see a task I want to put off each time. So, as a leader, I look for a way to delegate or eliminate it. Why run into a wall you don't have to? Look to hand-off essential things that drain you so you can focus on the big picture. But don't allow laziness to creep in and let your proverbial garden get infested by weeds.

Asking the Right Questions and Inviting the Right Perspective

Second, leading lean means asking the right questions up front. Your strategy is only as good as the data you're working from. If you have the wrong metrics, your targets are off from the start. To validate your starting place, inviting differing perspectives is of great help. This challenge sparks ideas and strengthens strategy. If you haven't tried to poke some holes in your strategies or tactics, you haven't put in all of the up-front work. This also helps you find places where miscommunication, not wrong thinking, is the problem.

Accountability

Third, accountability must be a core tenant. At the end of the day, someone is paying you money to produce results. So, ask yourself: "Am I achieving the results I'm being paid for?" The ride is over pretty quickly if you don't add more value than you take. When you do things the right way, though, people can't live without it. For the lean leader, accountability isn't a bad word, it's an opportunity to shine.

Leading In-House and Outsource Teams

These principles ripple into any team you lead. Whether you have a small in-house team or a broad array of outsource workers, they'll carry similar weight. Regardless of the kind or size of team you lead, you're going to face limited resources and head count at some point. When you model those characteristics and instill them in others, you'll get ever closer to maximum efficiency. And not just efficiency, but effectiveness. Doing work that is not impactful more efficiently, just means that you get the wrong things done more quickly!

Imagine a team who tackles projects by maximizing limited resources, avoiding burn out, communicating clearly, and is accountable for their own results. This is an unstoppable team. Because when you hit hurdles, you'll have the depth to figure them out. Whether remote or in-house, these qualities will carry your company through challenge. And also set you up for massive success when everything falls into place. Leading lean starts with you first. But the great news is, success and growth are contagious. So embody these principles and pass them on.

LEADING LEAN

Chapter Summary

In this final chapter, I overviewed what it means to lead lean—both for yourself and your team. Let's review what lean leadership is and how it's done, so you can increase your impact from the moment you close this book.

1. It's easy to help other people engage in lean principles without modeling them yourself.

2. Lean leadership means leading yourself in three primary ways: discipline, asking the right questions and inviting the right perspective, and being accountable for results.

3. If you don't make these constant habits, neither will your teams.

4. The team that brings these lean principles to the table will be unstoppable in the long-haul.

CONCLUSION

CONCLUSION

Becoming a Lean CMO requires a holistic approach to your business—but the rewards are tremendous.

The marketers who add more value than they take will always be in demand. And the Lean CMO is always positioned to do so. The concept of lean work, doing a lot with a little, is key for leaders in companies of every size. So whether you're the CMO of a Fortune 500 company, or a solopreneur working in the trenches on your own, these principles, habits, and practices won't let you down.

As with many things, though, the fastest way to grow is by learning from the failures and successes of people who've gone before you. I hope you found value in this book. I want to share my experiences and hard-earned insights with as many people as I can. Because I've seen these things work first-hand. And I've also lived through the consequences of ignoring them.

So, I invite you to connect with me, ask questions, and continue our conversation.

BOOK
DESCRIPTION

BOOK DESCRIPTION

The goal of every marketer is more sales. But achieving this on a consistent basis is tougher than ever in such a noisy marketplace. With a deep focus on engaging ideal prospects and inviting them closer to conversions, author Dwight Holcomb demystifies the black box of modern marketing.

In *The Lean CMO: How a Small Marketing Budget Can Produce Big Results,* Holcomb shows exactly how to get more with less.

Through his storied career and first-hand experience, you will learn how to maximize the value of your teams, tactics, and especially, yourself. And the best part is, you won't find a book filled with a high-dollar approach. Instead, you'll find a marketing system that's lean, smart, and brilliantly effective to the core.

Welcome to the guide that will transform you into a Lean CMO.

www.ingramcontent.com/pod-product-compliance
Lightning Source LLC
Chambersburg PA
CBHW071604200326
41519CB00021BB/6869